Discover Courage To Face Your Future

Discover Courage To Face Your Future

Robert H. Schuller

Harvest House Publishers
Irvine, California 92714

DISCOVER COURAGE TO FACE YOUR FUTURE

Copyright © 1978 by Robert H. Schuller
ISBN: 0-89081-156-3

*All rights reserved.
Printed in the United States of America.*

CONTENTS

Chapter One
Dare To Step Into Tomorrow 7

Chapter Two
The Past Can Be Changed 17

Chapter Three
The Courage To Face Your Future 29

1

Dare To Step Into Tomorrow

If I could give you one quality today by the grace and power of God it would be courage—the courage to take the step that can change your life! You can become a new you if you will dare to step into the tomorrow that God has planned for you!

I have to admit that the inspiration for my title came from a letter that I received from my good friend, Frank Sinatra. He sent me a beautiful long and personal letter and I'd like to share a few lines with you. He writes, "Dr. Schuller, your television messages are medicine to my mind. Somehow, every time I listen to your messages, I have the courage to step into tomorrow!" Those are powerful words! *You too can have the courage to step into tomorrow!*

8/DISCOVER COURAGE

We had a wonderful Christmas this past year except for one little problem. It rained. We have a cozy little mountain cottage up in Big Bear, California. My son

DARE TO STEP INTO TOMORROW/9

and I practically built it with our own hands, eleven years ago. Every winter we spend some time up there, enjoying the peace and quiet and the beautiful snow. But this Christmas we went up to our cabin and it was raining! There was no snow, just rain and mud slides. What a disappointment to everybody! And then, to top it off, our roof leaked! Water was dripping on my head as I tried to put pails under all the leaks.

Before long I became a little bit irritated and started preaching a sermon to the cabin. "This is disgusting!" I exclaimed. "Here I am with water dripping on my head and I can't even go outside because there it's pouring down rain! Don't you know who I am?" I asked, ignoring the stares of my family. I went on, "Remember when we first met? I was only a carpenter but now I am a preacher! And this cannot go on. I'm not going to come back here and spend another three days during the Christmas season and let you douse me with water." That little outburst really helped me for it relieved all the tension that was stored up inside!

When we got all the pails situated, I set about trying to find something for my two youngest girls to do. And I did something that I have never done before in my entire life. I took my children downtown to the only place where there was any action—THE ARCADE! What an experience! Lights were flashing and bells were ringing everywhere! I had never been in such a confusing place in my life. It was a mass of human beings, body to body, feeding quarters and nickels and dimes into machines.

"Girls!" I shouted, "We came to the mountains for peace and tranquility! This is too much! Let's get out of here!" But just as I turned to leave the Arcade I

DARE TO STEP INTO TOMORROW/11

spotted a tall blond haired young man standing on the opposite side of the room. He was very tall and appeared to be staring at me. I could see him pressing through the crowd, trying to get to me before I took off out the door. Suspecting that maybe he was a friend that had seen me on television I decided to wait until he reached me. He kept coming through the crowd as fast as he could until he was only five feet away from me.

The young man stared at me with intensity. I smiled and extended my hand. "Are you Reverend Schuller?" he asked as he warmly shook my hand. "Yes," I answered. "You're neat," he exclaimed. "Well, thank you," I said. Then he continued. "I watch you on television every Sunday. You've really changed my life!"

He was excited as he spoke to me. During the entire conversation we were standing in the middle of the Arcade

DARE TO STEP INTO TOMORROW/13

amidst the crowds and the noise, but neither of us seemed to notice.

"You have a mountain cabin up here, don't you?" he continued. "Why, yes," I replied. "And somebody broke in a couple of years ago and stole your television set, stereo and your son's skiis, right?" Now I was really confused. "How did you know?" I queried. "I'm the one who did it," he explained. "And I really feel bad about it. I was only 17 and I was a bad kid. But they caught us and you know all about that." "Yes," I replied, "I was asked to go to court and testify but I was out of town so the judge handled it without my coming up here." "I'm really sorry Dr. Schuller, but you did get all your things back undamaged, right?" he asked. "Yes, I went down to the police station to identify the stolen goods," I assured him.

Before my young friend left I had to ask

him, "How did you get into my cabin?" "Oh," he said, "it was easy. I climbed up the outside to the sliding glass door on the second level. Somebody had left it open. By the way," he added, "After the court proceeding somebody came up to me and said, 'Do you know who's cabin you ripped off?' And I said, 'No.' And my friend said, 'You broke into Dr. Schuller's place!' 'Oh, yea?' I exclaimed. 'Who's he?' 'He's the minister at the Garden Grove Community Church. He's on television every Sunday!' he explained. And that's when I started watching you on television!"

"Are you a Christian?" I asked. "I don't know, but I sure want to be. How do I become a Christian?" he responded. "Well," I said, "just exactly the way you are going about it. You go up to somebody who is a Christian and ask them! It begins by living your life with Jesus

Christ. You need to say: Dear Jesus Christ, I know I have sinned. You know that too. I need forgiveness. I need salvation. I need to be a more beautiful person. And I want you to come into my heart and mind and change me. I love you and I want to be like you."

"Would you like to offer that kind of a prayer?" I asked my young friend. "Sure," he enthusiastically replied. "We can do that right here and now if you don't mind," I said. "No, I don't mind," he enthused. And right there in the middle of the Arcade on Main Street in Big Bear, California, I offered a prayer and he repeated after me. Then we gave each other a hug.

"Do you have any Christian friends?" I asked. "Well," he said, "the kid that was with me when I broke into your cabin just recently found Jesus and he's going to a Bible group this week." "Good," I enthusiastically encouraged, "Go with him! And I'd like to send you some books for a daily, mental and spiritual treat, okay?"

I don't believe I've ever met a young man that had more courage than he did! It's unbelievable how human beings change! You can be a new you! Old or new, it's up to you! There's a great new you waiting to come through if you will take the right steps! You can have the courage to make the decision! God Almighty believes in you! When somebody believes in you and tells you they believe in you, before you know it, you begin to believe in yourself. The confidence that somebody else has in you becomes a self-fulfilling expectation that is placed on the subconscious level of your mind until your new expectation of yourself becomes literally a self-fulfilling prediction!

2

The Past Can Be Changed

A very good friend of mine stood in this pulpit one Sunday morning several years ago and delivered one of the most inspiring messages I have ever heard. Bill Sands is in heaven today but when he stood before this congregation—what a message he shared! I remember when, in the course of his message he put his finger on his nose and it totally flattened out. There was no cartilage left in Bill's nose because it had been beaten out by convicts in San Quentin prison. His nose has been flattened by led pipes and by the fists of tough guards.

It was on the second of July in 1941 that Bill Sands stood in the courtroom and heard the judge pronounce his sentence: Not less than one year nor more than life

18/DISCOVER COURAGE

in San Quentin! Months later, the word, INCORRIGIBLE was stamped on his file. Think of that word. What a negative, ghastly, destructive label! *INCORRIGIBLE!* He was not eligible for parole. He would never get out of prison! But then something happened. Clinton Duffy was appointed warden of San Quentin and soon after arrival, he paid Bill a visit. "Bill," Duffy said, in a grave but courteous tone. "How would you like these walls to melt like butter? Or how would you like the iron bars to turn into water so you could just walk out?" Bill looked up at Duffy and sarcastically said, "Duffy, who are you kidding? I know what is on my record. It says in bold red letters: *INCORRIGIBLE*—not eligible for parole." "Bill," Warden Duffy exclaimed, "that's true, but let me tell you something else. I believe in you! I believe you can become a new you! God can help you change." That

THE PAST CAN BE CHANGED/19

was the beginning of a new life for Bill Sands!

There is somebody who believes in you and that somebody is Jesus Christ! It takes courage to step into that new life and become a Christian. You'll be stepping into a new tommorow; a different culture; a different life-style; a different collection of friends. A lot of things will change! That's why it takes courage! And if there is one thing Jesus Christ wants to give you today, it is courage! Courage to step into tomorrow!

In 1921, Lewis Lawes became the warden at Sing Sing Prison. No prison was tougher than Sing Sing during that time. But when Warden Lawes retired 20 some years later, that prison had become a humanitarian institution. It was a model for other prisons to follow. Those who studied the system said credit for the change belonged to Lewis Lawes. But

20/DISCOVER COURAGE

when Warden Lawes was asked about the transformation, this is what he said: "I owe it all to my wonderful wife, Catherine, who is buried outside the prison walls."

Catherine Lawes was a young mother with three small children when her husband became the warden at Sing Sing prison. Everybody warned her from the beginning that she should never step foot inside the prison walls or in any other facility that the prisoners would be using, but that didn't stop Catherine! When the first prison basketball game was held she insisted on going. She walked into the auditorium with her three beautiful children and sat in the stands with the hardcore criminals. Other guests came up to her afterwards and asked, "How dare you sit with these men? Why do you take your little children in there?" And her reply was, "My husband and I are going

THE PAST CAN BE CHANGED/21

to take care of these men, and I believe they will take care of me! I don't have to worry!"

She even insisted on getting acquainted with the records of the men. She discovered that one of the men convicted of murder was blind, so she paid him a visit. She stepped into the cold cell and sat down next to this man. Holding his hand in hers she warmly said, "Do you read braille?" "What's braille?" he asked. "Don't you know? It is a way that you can read with your fingers," she explained. "Well, I've never heard of it," he replied. "I'll teach you then!" she enthused. And she taught that blind killer how to read braille. Years later he would weep in love for her.

Later Catherine found that there was a deaf mute in the prison, so she went to the school to learn sign language. Soon she was communicating with him through the use of her hands. Many said that Catherine Lawes was the body of Jesus Christ that came alive again at Sing Sing prison from 1921 to 1937.

Then one evening the car in which she was riding went out of control and she was killed. The next morning her husband did not come to work, so the acting warden came in his place. In an instant the whole prison knew something was wrong. When they heard the news that their beloved lady had died, everyone wept.

The following day her body was resting in a casket in her home, three quarters of a mile from the prison. As the acting warden took his early morning walk, he was shocked to see a large crowd of the toughest, hardest-looking criminals gathering like a herd of animals at the main gate. It looked as if they were ready to launch a riot. He walked over to the group and instead of seeing hositility in their eyes he saw tears of grief and sadness. He knew how much they loved and admired Catherine. He turned and faced the men. "Alright men, you can go. Just be sure and check in!" Then he opened the gate without another word and a parade of more than 100 criminals walked, without a guard, three quarters of a mile to stand in line to pay their respects to Catherine Lawes. And every one of them checked in that night. *Everyone! It's amazing what one life can do when it has the Spirit of Christ within.* Catherine Lawes believed there were no hopeless cases, only hopeless thinkers!

The warden's wife had the courage to take her little children and sit among murderers and rapists; a blond boy ripped off the house of a preacher two years ago, but had the courage to admit what he did and ask for forgiveness. Do you have courage? How much nerve do you

THE PAST CAN BE CHANGED/25

have? Do you have enough courage to trust God as He comes to you and says: "I believe in you! I have a dream for your life!" Do you have the courage to step into tomorrow? Do you dare to step into the future? God is there waiting with Jesus Christ and He wants to tell you what a beautiful person you can become.

Let me tell you something. I made a discovery 22 years ago while ringing doorbells in this community. My wife was the only member and we wanted to start a church. We picked a slogan: A church that can put strong wings on weary hearts.

I would ring a doorbell and ask, "Are you an active member of a local church?" They would say, "Yes, we go to the Methodist Church. Then I would say, "Good, God bless you. Keep on going, they need every member they can get." Then I'd go to the next house and ask the same question. And they would say, "Yes, we go to the local Roman Catholic Church." "Good," I would say, "They need every member they can get." Or they would say, "We go to the Jewish Synagogue."

Then I would come to a house and ask once again, "Are you an active member of a local church?" And they would say, "No we don't belong to a church." And then I would say, "Do you have a faith?" And they would say, "No." And that's when I got to talk to them about Jesus Christ! They would usually invite me in and I would quickly look around. The house was generally neat, the lawn was kept up and the furnishings were nice. And as I looked into their eyes I saw beautiful people! I would look into the faces of these beautiful people and ask, "Why does a beautiful person like you not go to church?" They would usually come up with some excuse or say that

THE PAST CAN BE CHANGED/27

they just never discovered it. That's when I had a revelation.

God said to me: "Robert Schuller, you are a Christian. The person you just talked to is not a Christian. Let me tell you that being a Christian does not mean that you are a better person than a non-Christian." That was kind of shocking! The second revelation was: "Bob, many non-Christian people are more beautiful than some Christian church members." And I accepted that. And then God said: "But, Schuller, you are a more beautiful person today because you are a Christian than if you were not a Christian! And these people, who are beautiful people even though they are non-Christians, will become even more beautiful if they will accept Jesus Christ into their lives."

Any person will become a more beautiful person if he accepts Jesus Christ into his life. I invite you to dare to step forward and accept Jesus Christ. We are still in the early flush of a new year. Decide now to walk with Christ!

3

The Courage To Face Your Future

I want to ask you three questions. They were inspired by God when I was called upon to deliver a message at Hubert Humphrey's funeral. The questions have a universal application. First of all, what is courage? Second, why do we exalt courage? And third, where can you get it?

I.
What is courage?

We can all understand what courage is when we see a soldier fighting for our freedom as he heads for the front line. We can understand courage when we see a fire truck speeding down the street and the fireman climbing his ladder. We can understand courage when we see the police officer rushing through the black of night to protect someone from being assaulted by a mad man. That is a form of courage that we can all understand.

The Bible exalts that kind of courage! The words, "fear not" appear in the Bible 365 times. Once for every day of the year!

But there are different types and levels of courage. There is, of course, the courage to love. It takes a great deal of courage to love because when you really love someone you become emotionally involved and that means you've made a choice! You have made an emotional commitment. Now you are committed to something and you run the risk of being rejected. People often ask me, "Dr. Schuller, why isn't there more love in the world?" And my immediate reply is, "You are asking the wrong question. The right question to ask is, "Why don't more people dare to love?" It takes courage to love because when you love you get involved! And when you do that, you are liable to be swept away, and before you realize it, you've made a deep commitment!

There are many people, today, who are afraid of marriage. People are living together instead of going through the marriage ceremony. They offer several reasons for their behavior, but at a deeper level, they are afraid of marriage because they are afraid to make a commitment to continuity. *It takes courage to love!* Ultimately, love is going to have to lead to a commitment. Love is shallow until you are willing to make a commitment to continuity—to love even when the skin is wrinkled and the hair is white! It takes courage to love!

Another form of courage is the courage to forgive! You will not love long if you cannot forgive quickly. In all of our interpersonal relationships, we will not love long unless we have the capacity to forgive quickly. That includes my love for God. Forgive God? Yes. There are people today who are atheists because at the deepest level they are really angry at God. Maybe as children they cried out and didn't get what they thought God should have given them, so they became angry towards Him. Or perhaps they experienced a crisis in a personal relationship and they cried out to God, asking for something but God appeared to be silent. They've never really brought themselves to a point where they are willing to forgive God and start over again.

When you forgive, you are not saying that the other party has done anything wrong. That's why you can forgive God. Because forgiveness means you are able to accept what comes your way. It's easy to forgive somebody if they are guilty and they repent, but it's not easy to accept

COURAGE TO FACE YOUR FUTURE/33

some things that life puts before you. That kind of forgiveness takes courage. To love requires courage! It takes courage to forgive and unless you are able to forgive quickly, your love will never last long in any relationship.

Some of you may harbor a resentment against a husband, wife, child, teacher, or maybe an employer. You just don't dare to forgive. Part of it is the fact that if you really forgave that person, you'd have to swallow your pride. Only brave people dare to be humble! It takes courage to love. It takes courage to forgive because you see, you run the risk of rejection, ridicule and scorn from those whose scales of justice are too heavy and scales of mercy are too light.

What is courage? Well, we can now understand the courage of the fireman and policeman; the courage of the husband and wife who go to the altar to make a permanent commitment; and the courage of forgiveness. But there is another level of courage that I could not understand for a long time. This was the courage of a person who bravely fights a terminal illness. My secretary died of cancer after battling it for twelve years. I remember people saying to me, "Bob, Lois is so brave," and I have never really understood that statement.

I first met Hubert Humphrey about five years ago. I received a letter from him saying that he and his wife, Muriel, watched the Hour of Power and that it was a great help to them on a very deep and personal level. He told me to stop in and see him the next time I was in Washington so I did! When I found his office I told his secretary who I was and she smiled and said, "Oh, Dr. Schuller, he really wants to see you!" Then she had a member of his staff take me to the Senate

Chamber where Senator Humphrey was speaking.

He was finishing just as I entered the room. When he rushed over and warmly embraced me, I didn't know exactly what to say, so I handed him one of the little gold cards with the possibility thinkers creed printed on it. "What's this?" Hubert asked. And I told him to read it. In his strong and sturdy voice he began reading:

> When faced with a mountain I will not quit, I will keep on striving until I climb over, find a pass through, tunnel underneath or simply stay and turn the mountain into a gold mine, with God's help.

Tears filled his eyes before he could finish. This was only the beginning of what would become a deep, personal relationship.

People have said it through the years and I affirm it today—Hubert had great courage! People who fight a terminal illness, and keep on fighting bravely, have courage! I have always admired their perseverance. I have always admired their faith. But I used to say, "Why do you call it courage? What's so brave about it? Perseverance? Yes. Tough? Of course. But courageous? But why do you say it's courage when somebody's fighting a battle of cancer?"

It's courageous because a person who fights a brave battle with a terminal illness, is making a commitment! There can be no courage unless there is a choice between alternatives. And the person who is fighting a terminal illness is making a choice between two alternatives. One is to overdose and slip away quickly. The other is to hang in there as bravely and optimistically as possible until God stops the heartbeat. When you're faced with alternatives, choose the one where the personal price is high, but where the reward in terms of inspiration to those around you is also high. That's courage!

II.

Why do we exalt courage?

Because every person who chooses to be brave inspires the rest of the human race! That's why! The entire human family, is exalted, honored, and dignified as a species when some other fellow creature fights their brave battle and we can say, "That's my relative or that's my friend!"

In my recent book, *Peace of Mind Through Possibility Thinking,* I tell about a conversation I had with a good friend, Abby. She writes her own column in the newspaper, called "Dear Abby." We were at dinner together in Beverly Hills and I was telling her about our ministry and the suicides that we prevent through our 24 hour, life-line, Christian, telephone counseling program. She was surprised when I told her that we operate the longest standing, continually operating, New Hope Telephone Counseling Center right here on the campus of the Garden Grove Community Church. I told her how proud we were of the fact that no ministry saves more lives than we do!

Abby's reply was a question, "Dr. Schuller, what's so wrong about suicide?" "What's wrong with suicide," I replied, "is that it's the easy way out. Your friends and relatives are the ones left behind to live with the terrible hurt. They carry the scars for the rest of their lives!"

Your life and mine will be judged before Almighty God on this question: "When I was faced with alternatives did I choose the brave way?" And if I did, I

COURAGE TO FACE YOUR FUTURE/39

uplifted the collective level of social self-esteem in the process. That's why we exalt courage!

I have never met Charlotte Valente but I sure want to some day. I became acquainted with her story through some literature that I received from the Children's Hospital in Los Angeles.

Mary Ames Anderson, now the retired editor said if she were to pick one child in the Children's Hospital that inspired her more than anybody else, it would have to be Charlotte Valente. And here's Mary Anderson's beautiful story.

"I was walking through the corridor of the children's hospital in 1953 when I heard a young voice say, 'Here I am!' I stopped and turned to see where the voice was coming from. And that's when I saw a little girl, barely two years old, lying in bed hugging her teddy bear. She seemed so young to be speaking so clearly. Both of her tiny legs were hanging in the air, in traction. 'Well, hello!' I enthused. Smiling, she asked, 'How are you today?' But before I could answer she interrupted, 'I have brittle bones. This one is broken. Last time it was that one,' she said as she pointed to her right leg. 'But this time it is this one. I have had 22 fractures!'

"By the age of six Charlotte had been in and out of the hospital 85 times. She has a rare disease which causes her bones to break very easily. She had over 200 fractures by the time she was ten but she is a delightful little girl, always smiling and very positive.

"I only saw her cry three time," Mrs. Anderson wrote. "Once when she fractured her arm the day before her sister's wedding and she had to stay in the hospital. The other time was when she made a community appeal to urge people to give so crippled children could walk. 'I will never walk,' Charlotte said in her plea, 'but hundreds of others can walk if only you'll help!' Charlotte couldn't walk because by the time she reached puberty the disease arrested itself and her normal development had been permanently distorted. She would probably never weigh more than fifty pounds in her entire lifetime. But this brave young girl didn't cry until she was recognized by community leaders. And do you know why? Because they gave her a typewriter—the one material thing that she'd wanted ever since she was a child. She didn't want a bike because she could never ride one. She wanted a typewriter! And when she was presented this gift she cried and cried. 'I'm the luckiest girl in the whole world!' she exclaimed." *That's courage!*

Charlotte went on to high school and graduated. Then she picked a university that had ramps equipped for the handicapped. She was accepted and graduated four years later Cum Laude! But Charlotte did not stop there! She went on to law school and passed the state bar exam. All 50 pounds of her!

Courage! What is it? It's the back side of love. That's what it is. It's the other side of the coin. Somebody who loves life enough to want to live every minute no matter how costly it may be! Somebody so much in love with life that he will fight everyday through the pain of chemotherapy and radiation. Somebody who loves persons enough to be willing to say, "I take you for better, for worse, for richer or poorer, in sickness and in health, till death do us part." Somebody who loves God enough to believe that He will never abandon you!

III.

Where do you get this kind of courage?

You get it from the Ideal One more than anywhere else. At a very deep level this is what you and I need. I have it and I hope I can share it with you. We all need an Ideal One! One ideal person who lives in our minds and loves us. One to whom we can relate. One who lifts us and inspires us. And for me, that Ideal One is Jesus Christ!

What happens to a human being who carries within his mind some person who is Perfect and Ideal? The love of life comes in and that brings courage! The late Ozzie Nelson used to tell this story about his son, Ricky.

He said, "Ricky was just a young boy when he begged me to let his friend, Walter come over and spend the weekend with him. After much persistence I gave in. On the day that Walter was to come over I got off work a little early so I could play with the boys. We went into the backyard and started throwing a football around. I was getting really good

COURAGE TO FACE YOUR FUTURE/45

when Ricky said, 'Hey, dad, you're great!' And Walter piped in and exclaimed, 'Gee, Mr. Nelson, you've got a pretty good arm, but not as good as my dad.' When it came to dinnertime I carved the roast so beautifully with thin and even slices. 'Look at those nice slices, Walter,' I bragged. 'You carve the roast pretty good, Mr. Nelson,' Walter enthused, 'but you should see my dad do it!' I couldn't believe it! I couldn't do anything as well as this kid's father.

"Well, when their bedtime came I decided to tell one of my best stories. Their eyes were popping out of their heads! 'That's a great story, Mr. Nelson, but my dad is one of the best storytellers there is!' And the next day the same thing happened, no matter what we did together. I was starting to dislike a man I'd never even met. I couldn't wait for Walter's mother to pick him up so I could find out about this super-dad! When she came to

the door I said, 'Hi! I'm delighted to meet you.' 'How was Walter?' she asked. 'Oh, just great,' I exclaimed, 'I'd sure like to meet your husband. He must be something else!' 'Oh, no,' she said, 'has Walter been talking about his dad again? You see, Walter was only three years old when his dad was killed at Corregidor.' "
That little boy had an Ideal One that lived within him. His image of his father gave him courage.

My Ideal One died before I was born—at Calvary! But He lives today! His name is Jesus! That's where I get my courage. That's where I get my nerve. He lives in me and He wants to live in you!

Notes

Notes